W9-CNF-934

WITHDRAWN

Mice

TEXT BY ELAINE PASCOE

PHOTOGRAPHS BY DWIGHT KUHN

BLACKBIRCH PRESS

An imprint of Thomson Gale, a part of The Thomson Corporation

THOMSON ™

GALE

Detroit • New York • San Francisco • San Diego • New Haven, Conn. • Waterville, Maine • London • Munich

3 1267 13939 0916

© 2005 Thomson Gale, a part of The Thomson Corporation.

Thomson and Star Logo are trademarks and Gale and Blackbirch Press are registered trademarks used herein under license.

For more information, contact
Blackbirch Press
27500 Drake Rd.
Farmington Hills, MI 48331–3535
Or you can visit our Internet site at http://www.gale.com

ALL RIGHTS RESERVED
No part of this work covered by the copyright hereon may be reproduced or used in any form or by any means—graphic, electronic, or mechanical, including photocopying, recording, taping, Web distribution or information storage retrieval systems—without the written permission of the publisher.

Every effort has been made to trace the owners of copyrighted material.

Photo Credits: All photos, including cover © Dwight Kuhn

LIBRARY OF CONGRESS CATALOGING–IN–PUBLICATION DATA

Pascoe, Elaine.
  Mice / by Elaine Pascoe. Photography by Dwight Kuhn.
    p. cm. — (Nature close–up)
  Includes bibliographical references and index.
  ISBN 1–4103–0537–6 (hard cover : alk. paper)
  1. Mice—Juvenile literature. I. Title.

QL737.R6P28 2005
599.35'3—dc22   2005007650

Contents

1 A World of Mice   **4**

   Nonstop Gnawers   5

   Country Mice   8

   City Mice   11

   More Mice   13

   Life Cycle   16

   Mice and People   20

2 Keeping and Caring for Mice   **24**

   Pet Mice   25

   Mouse House   26

   Care and Handling   28

3 Investigating Mice   **32**

   Where Do Mice Like to Nest?   33

   What Nesting Materials Do Mice Like? 34

   Tunnel or Hole?   36

   How Do Mice Prefer to Drink?   38

   More Activities with Mice   40

   Results and Conclusions   41

Some Words About Mice   **45**

For More Information   **47**

Index   **48**

1

A World of Mice

It's night. The house is quiet. But as you lie in bed, you hear a faint scratching noise. The sound seems to come from somewhere behind your bedroom wall. It's a mouse!

Most people think of mice as pests—and when mice get into our homes, they are pests. But these little animals do not entirely deserve their bad reputation. Mice have an important role in nature, and they are fascinating to watch. They are also among the most successful animals, thriving in different **habitats** all over the world.

Mice and rats belong to the same animal family. Size is the main difference between rats and mice. People call the large members of the family rats and the smaller members mice. In all there are more than 1,300 different species in this family, accounting for about 30 percent of all the known kinds of **mammals**.

Nonstop Gnawers

The many different kinds of mice have certain traits in common. Like all mammals, they have hair. They are warm–blooded, which means their body temperature stays the same when the outside temperature changes. Mice give birth to live young, and they nurse their young with milk that the mothers produce.

Mice belong to a group of mammals called **rodents**. Squirrels, beavers, porcupines, hamsters, guinea pigs, and many other small animals belong to this group. The name rodent comes from a Latin word that means "to gnaw," and that is what rodents do. Like other rodents, a mouse has four sharp gnawing teeth—two in the upper jaw and two in the lower jaw. The teeth look like little chisels. They grow throughout the animal's lifetime, but they are constantly worn away as the animal chews. The teeth have hard enamel on the front, but they are softer in back. Thus, the back edge wears away faster, leaving a sharp edge in front.

A mouse keeps its front teeth sharp by gnawing.

5

Mice share a basic body shape, with a pointed nose, round ears, and a long tail. Their short, thick fur is usually gray or brown. Like cats, mice clean their fur with their tongues. Their front legs are short, and they use the front paws like hands to hold food. The hind legs are longer and stronger than the front legs. Mice are excellent climbers and, with their strong hind legs, good jumpers.

A deer mouse scurries around the base of a tree to escape a predator.

The silky pocket mouse lives in the desert.

Mice also have keen senses of smell and hearing. These senses help them find food and mates and avoid the many **predators**, from cats to birds of prey, that eat mice. Many mice also use their sense of smell to find their way to and from their nests. They travel along trails that they mark with their urine, using the scent to follow the trails. Mice can hear sounds—including the squeaks and trills of other mice—that are higher in pitch than the sounds people can hear.

A mouse's eyesight is not as sharp as its other senses are. But mice have large eyes that help them see in the dark, and their long whiskers help them feel their way. That is

helpful because most mice are **nocturnal**. They sleep during the day and are active at night.

Some mice are mainly plant eaters. They are especially fond of fruit, seeds, and nuts. Many mice also eat insects, centipedes, snails, or other small animals and whatever else they can find. They are **onmivorous**—they eat a bit of everything. Unlike mice in cartoons, real mice are not crazy for cheese.

Country Mice

The most common mice native to North America are the white-footed mouse and the deer mouse. It is hard to tell these two species apart. Both are small. They are typically about 6 inches (15cm) long including the tail, which makes up almost half their body's length. Both species have big ears, big black eyes, and fur resembling a deer's fur—brown or grayish brown on the back and white on the legs and underside. In deer mice, this coloring continues along the tail, which is dark on top and light below. The tail of the white-footed mouse does not have a

Mice are excellent jumpers.

sharp color division. White-footed mice may also have redder coats than deer mice have, but not always.

Outside cities, white-footed and deer mice are found almost everywhere—in forests, fields, and brush. They are seldom seen, because they are shy and nocturnal. They spend the day in small, cuplike nests that they make under rocks or stumps, in hollow logs or

A white-footed mouse makes a nest of grasses.

other cavities, or among debris. They sometimes nest in sheds or houses, especially if people seldom use the buildings. They line their nests with soft materials such as plant fibers and feathers.

At night, white-footed and deer mice scurry around looking for food. You may hear them rustling through fallen leaves or, if you listen closely, drumming their feet on the ground. The mice gather seeds and berries, stuff them into their cheeks, and take them back to their nests to eat later. They also eat plant buds, insects, spiders, and other small animals. They eat a lot for their size. A deer mouse may eat half its body weight in food each day.

These mice spend their whole lives within a small **home range**, making trails as they go about their search for

Berries are a winter treat for a white-footed mouse.

food. Depending on how much food they can find, the range may be no bigger than a backyard. They do not **hibernate** in winter. Instead, they survive by eating seeds that they stored in the fall. They also continue to search for food, making tunnels under the snow. You can sometimes see the maze–like patterns of their tunnels as the snow melts.

City Mice

The house mouse is the most common mouse in cities. House mice are not native to North America. Like their much bigger cousins, Norway (brown) rats, they arrived long ago aboard ships from Europe. The mice probably stowed away in shipments of grain or other goods. In this way, house mice have spread throughout much of the world.

A young deer mouse collects berries.

The house mouse is found wherever people live.

House mice are slightly smaller than deer mice, and they have smaller eyes. They are brownish gray, so they blend in with shadows. Their ears and scaly tails are almost hairless. House mice are seldom found far from humans. In houses and other buildings, they build their nests between walls and in attics or other unused spaces. Like deer mice, house mice are seldom seen. If mice are in the house, you may hear them scratching and gnawing in the walls at night. You also may see their droppings, which look like tiny black seeds, in areas where food is kept.

House mice are excellent climbers and can run up any rough vertical surface. They can also jump more than a foot (31 cm) in height, and they can run along ropes and cables like tightrope walkers. Any crack big enough to fit a pencil is big enough for house mice to squeeze through. In this way the mice roam the house at night, searching for food. They love cereal and other grains, but they will eat whatever food they can find—including garbage.

More Mice

House mice are found almost anywhere that people live. Many other kinds of mice live only in certain habitats, where they can find the food and other conditions that they need. Among the most fascinating mice are grasshopper mice. Small but stocky, grasshopper mice are found in brushy areas and grasslands in the western United States. They are hunters that stalk and kill insects, scorpions, spiders, and other small animals— even other small rodents.

A grasshopper mouse's front teeth are shaped more like daggers than chisels. The mouse ambushes its **prey**, leaping out and killing it with a quick bite to the neck. Then it eats its kill from the head down. These fierce little mice have been called "wolves in mouse clothing." They even stand on their hind legs and howl like tiny wolves!

Harvest mice are common in farm fields. They are quite small, often just 4 to 6 inches (10 to 15 cm) long. They are dark brown on top and lighter brown below. Harvest mice are mainly seedeaters, but they also eat sprouts and some insects. They gather seeds on the ground or by bending plant stalks to bite off the seed heads. Harvest mice weave baseball–size grass nests in shrubs or among grasses.

Voles, which are sometimes called field mice, belong to a different branch of the mouse family. There are many vole species. Meadow voles are about the same length as deer mice overall, but their tails are shorter and their bodies are larger. Their eyes are smaller, too, and their dense brown fur often hides their ears.

Meadow voles live in pastures, roadsides, farm fields, and other grassy or weedy sites, often near water. They make networks of trails along the ground, clipping the plants along these paths. Underground, they make tunnels and chambers for nesting and storing food. Voles are mostly plant eaters. They feed on grasses and other plants, and in winter they eat the bark and roots of trees. They are not good climbers and do not usually enter homes.

Opposite page: A meadow vole chews on the bark of a tree. This page: Meadow voles live in grassy areas. They seldom enter houses.

Newborn white-footed mice are tiny, hairless, and blind.

Life Cycle

Most mice breed often and have lots of offspring. Sheltered from the weather, the house mouse breeds as often as every ten weeks throughout the year. Deer mice usually have two to four litters a year. They breed most often during warm weather and when food is in good supply. The females give birth about three weeks after breeding. There may be as many as nine pups in a litter, but the average litter size is about five. Females raise their young alone—the males do not help.

Newborn mice are blind, deaf, and hairless, except for their whiskers. Each pup weighs only about $\frac{1}{25}$ ounce (1g) at birth. The young nurse almost constantly, and they grow fast. Deer mouse pups begin to grow grayish fur and double in size in the first week. In two weeks, their eyes are open and they are moving around. Their waste soon make the nest damp and dirty. The mother solves this problem by building a new nest and moving the pups to it. She carries them with her mouth, one by one. When the new nest is soiled, she moves the pups again.

At three to four weeks, deer mouse pups are **weaned**. The mother stops nursing them, and she leaves the nest. Now the young mice must find their own food. They spend a

A mother mouse cleans her newborn young.

By the time they are 18 days old, the young mice have soft gray fur.

few more weeks near the nest, as they explore and search for food. By the time they are eight weeks old, they are ready to breed and raise their own litters. They leave to make nests of their own.

If each female mouse raises several litters a year, and all her female pups raise litters of their own, mouse populations can grow fast. Food supply and weather limit the growth, however. So do predators. Mice are a major food for coyotes, foxes, weasels, skunks, snakes, owls and other birds of prey, and many other animals. Thus, many mice do not live long enough to breed. Even those that escape predators do not live very long. One or two years is a ripe old age for most mice, although some types live longer.

A saw–whet owl swoops down to catch a mouse.

Mice and People

The link between mice and people goes back thousands of years. Not long after people first began to grow and store grain, mice showed up to steal it. The ancestors of modern house mice left their wild habitats and moved in alongside people to be close to their new food supply. Wild mice still enter peoples' homes in search of food. Many house mice are so used to life with people, they would have trouble surviving in the wild.

As long as mice have been stealing food from people, people have been trying to stop them. There are good reasons to keep mice out of the house. Besides eating food supplies, mice soil countertops and other surfaces with their waste. They carry and spread diseases. With their constant gnawing, they can damage everything from stored clothing to the walls of houses.

This young deer mouse has found a tasty snack in someone's kitchen.

20

POCKET MICE

At first glance, a pocket mouse looks like any other mouse. Actually, this little rodent is more closely related to squirrels than to true mice. It is named for the fur–lined cheek pouches that open alongside its mouth. The pocket mouse uses these external cheek pouches to carry its food.

Pocket mice are native to western North America and parts of South America. There are more than 30 different kinds. Most types found in the United States, such as the plains pocket mouse and the silky pocket mouse, are quite small, just 4 to 5 inches (10 to 12cm) long. Pocket mice have long hind legs and are great jumpers. Some kinds have soft fur, and some have stiff spines mixed in with their fur.

Most pocket mice live in deserts and other dry regions. They eat mainly seeds, and they can go without water for long periods. They nest in underground burrows, which they line with soft grass. During the day, they plug the openings to their burrows with dirt to keep out snakes. Like true mice, pocket mice are hunted by many predators. If they escape being eaten, they may live as long as five years.

*A pocket mouse leaves
its burrow at night.*

People have used everything from traps to poison to house cats to control mice. One of the best mouse–control methods is to keep all food out of their reach. Put cereal and other foods in mouse–proof containers. Clean kitchen counters, so there are no crumbs to attract mice. Put garbage in cans with tight–fitting lids.

A house cat on mouse patrol.

Some mice are specially bred for use in research or, like this one, as pets.

As pests, mice get a lot of bad press. But mice also do a lot of good. Wild mice eat large quantities of weed seeds and insect pests. Tame mice have been used for scientific research for more than 100 years, and they are the most widely used laboratory animals today. Scientists have bred different kinds of lab mice for specific research studies, but they are all descended from house mice.

Mice are also great pets. Like lab mice, pet mice are descendants of house mice. There are many types, including fancy types that are raised for show.

Keeping and Caring for Mice

Mice are quite shy, and they are mostly active at night. This makes them hard to observe. It is rare to catch more than a glimpse of a mouse in the wild. Pet mice behave like their wild cousins in many ways. By observing them, you can learn a lot about how these animals live in the wild. You can study behavior, feeding habits, reproduction, and many other aspects of mouse life with pet mice.

Pet Mice

Buy pet mice at a pet store. Wild mice seldom make good pets. They belong in their natural habitats, and it is best to leave them there. Wild mice also may carry diseases.

Most pet stores sell white mice, and many stores have a variety of types. You may find fancy mice, which are twice the size of ordinary pet mice. Fancy mice come in many different colors—from silver to cinnamon—and coat types, including longhaired, curly, and extra–glossy (satin). All the different kinds are descended from house mice. They may look different, but they behave in the same basic ways.

Mice like company, so it is fine to have several. Overcrowding leads to fighting and health problems, though. Do not put too many mice together. You can keep three to four mice in a 10–gallon (38l) aquarium. Females live especially well in groups. Males may fight if they are put together as adults. If they are introduced to each other when they are young, they generally get along. If a male mouse is aggressive, he should be separated from the others.

Do not put males and females together unless you want them to mate and have pups. Pet mice can have litters every six to eight weeks, so you may quickly have a lot of mice on your hands! Baby mice can be sold to pet stores, but they are usually resold as food for snakes and other animals.

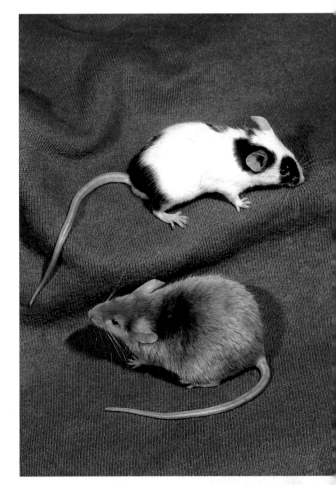

Pet mice come in many colors, but they are all descended from house mice.

Mouse House

An aquarium makes a good home for mice. They cannot gnaw it, and it is easy to clean. If you use an aquarium, you will need to put a wire rodent cover on top to keep the mice from escaping. Put several inches of bedding in the bottom of the aquarium. Use aspen or hardwood shavings or shredded paper products. Do not use cedar or pine shavings. These contain oils that irritate a mouse's eyes and skin.

For pet mice, an aquarium needs a wire lid. The mice will need water, food, toys, and bedding.

You also can keep mice in a wire cage, but be sure it is designed for mice. Mice may be able to squeeze between the bars of cages designed for hamsters and other small pets. Mice also like to dig up their bedding, often scattering it through the bars of the cage.

Mice are active and curious, so give them things to play with. Pet stores sell exercise wheels, climbing branches, and mouse toys. Mice also like cardboard tubes, which they can run through, and small boxes or flower pots, which they can hide in. Give them a small log or a piece of untreated, unpainted wood to chew. This will help keep their teeth short and satisfy their need to gnaw.

Give mice toys to climb on and crawl through.

Care and Handling

Give mice water in a water bottle or water tube, attached to the side of the mouse home, rather than a dish. Change the water every day. Give food twice a day in a ceramic or metal bowl. Mice will chew plastic bowls.

Water in a bottle stays clean, and the mice can't spill it.

28

Mice like seeds, and many enjoy fruits such as grapes.

Seed mixtures, pellets, and feed blocks especially made for rodents make a good basic diet. Many mice also enjoy small bits of fresh fruit and vegetables as treats. Try peas, carrots, apples, and bananas. Do not feed your mice cabbage, chocolate, corn, candy, junk food, peanuts, uncooked beans, or onions. All of these can cause health problems.

An old log, full of holes, makes a great mouse toy.

Remove droppings, uneaten food, and soiled bedding from the mouse house daily. Once a week, take out all the bedding, wipe down the inside of the container, and put in fresh bedding.

If pet mice are handled daily, they quickly become tame and rarely bite. Mice are easily frightened, though, so let them get used to handling slowly. At first, put your hand in the mouse house and let the mouse come to you. When the mouse is used to your hand, you can pick it up. Do this by gently scooping the mouse up from the belly. Do not grab it by the tail; this can hurt the mouse.

You can train a mouse to sit quietly in your hand by feeding it small treats. Remember that mice are good jumpers, though. Do not let it jump out of your hand. Handle the mouse in a safe place, where it will not be able to escape. Pet mice do not know how to survive on their own. They may starve or be eaten by predators.

With good care, pet mice may live one to three years. If you cannot keep your mice anymore, take them back to a pet store or find someone to adopt them.

Pet mice become tame with regular handling. Always hold mice gently.

Investigating Mice

Pet mice are excellent subjects for close–up study. In this chapter, you will find activities that will help you learn more about their ways. Have fun with these activities. Always handle your mice gently to avoid hurting or frightening them.

Where Do Mice Like to Nest?

Wild mice build nests in many different places. If your pet mice had a choice, what sort of nest site would they choose: one with a wide entry for easy access, or one with a small entry? Based on what you know about mice, decide what you think. Then do this activity to see if you are right.

What You Need:
• Cardboard to make nest boxes
• Nesting material such as hardwood shavings or shredded paper
• Mice
• Mouse house

What to Do:

1. Cut and fold cardboard to make a nest box with three compartments, separated by cardboard dividers (see photo). The box should fit along one side of the mouse house. The compartments should all be the same size.
2. Give each nest box a different opening. In the front of one, cut an entrance hole 1 inch (2.5 cm) across. In the front of the second, cut a hole 1.5 inches (4 cm) across. Make the front of the third box completely open.
3. Put nesting material in the boxes. Use the same type and amount of bedding in each.
4. Watch the mice to see where they nest.

Results: Do the mice prefer one box to the others? Repeat the activity, changing the order of the box fronts. Are your results the same?

Conclusion: Based on your results, what sites do you think mice prefer for nesting? How would their choice help them survive in the wild?

What You Need:
- At least four nesting materials
- Mouse house
- Container
- Mice

What Nesting Materials Do Mice Like?

In the wild, mice use natural materials in their nests. In homes, mice have been known to use the insulation in walls as nesting material! What sort of materials do you think they like best? Decide what you think, and then do this activity to see if you are right.

What to Do:

1. Put a large bunch of a different nesting material in each corner of the mouse house. You can use such things as yarn, dry leaves, shredded newspaper, and bedding from a pet store.

2. Watch to see what the mice do.

Results: Did the mice pick one material over the others for their nests? Try the experiment again with different materials. For example, use cotton batting, sand, dried grass or straw, and hardwood shavings.

Conclusion: Based on your results, what kinds of materials do mice prefer for nesting? Why do you think those materials appeal to mice?

What You Need:
- Two cardboard tubes from paper-towel rolls
- Aluminum foil
- Rubber band
- Mouse house
- Mice

Tunnel or Hole?

Mice are great explorers, in their quiet way. Do you think a mouse will enter a blocked tunnel as willingly as an open tunnel? Make your best guess, and then do this activity to find out.

What to Do:

1. Cover one end of one tube with a piece of aluminum foil and secure the foil with a rubber band. Leave the other end open. Leave both ends of the second tube open.

2. Put both tubes in the mouse house. Watch to see what the mice do.

Results: Note how the mice react to the tubes. Which tube do they enter more often?

Conclusion: What do your results tell you about the way mice get around in the wild?

What You Need:

- Water bottle
- Ceramic or metal dish
- Sponge
- Spray bottle
- Water
- Mouse house
- Mice

How Do Mice Prefer to Drink?

Pet mice usually get water from bottles in their cages. Wild mice do not have water bottles. If mice have a choice, how do they like to get their water? Decide what you think, based on what you know about mice. Then do this activity to see if you are right.

38

What to Do:

1. Fill the water bottle and attach it to the side of the mouse house.
2. Put the sponge in the dish, add water, and place it in the mouse house.
3. Using the spray bottle, mist one inside wall of the mouse house with water. (If you have a cage instead of an aquarium, spray water on dishes or other objects in the cage.)
4. Watch the mice to see where they drink.

Results: Note each time you see a mouse taking water from the bottle, the dish, or the misted area. Keep count to see which method they prefer.

Conclusion: Based on your results, what water sources do you think mice prefer? How do they get water in the wild?

More Activities with Mice

1. Watch a pet mouse over a few days. Make a chart to record your observations. Is your mouse more active during the day or night? When does it eat? What toys does it like best?

2. Conduct a mouse taste test to see what foods mice like. Try dog biscuits, birdseed, cereal, grapes, and other foods.

3. Find out where mice like to walk. Place a mouse in an empty aquarium. (You can line the bottom with paper, so you can easily clean up any mess it makes.) Watch the mouse for 30 minutes and note where it is each minute. Is it in the middle of the aquarium or next to a wall? When you are done, look over your observations to see where the mouse spent most of

its time. If you were setting a trap for a house mouse in your kitchen, in what part of the room would you place the trap?

Results and Conclusions

Here are some possible results and conclusions for the activities on pages 33 to 41. Many factors may affect the results of these activities. If your results differ, try to think of reasons why. Repeat the activity with different conditions, and see if your results change.

Where Do Mice Like to Nest?
Mice like the security of being undercover. As long as they feel secure and have a lot of nesting material to cover up with, they may not care about the opening to the nest site. However, our mice preferred the boxes with smaller

Hardwood or aspen shavings make good bedding for a pet mouse.

openings to the box with the open front. In the wild, a small opening would help keep out predators.

What Nesting Materials Do Mice Like?

Our mice were equally happy with yarn, dry leaves, shredded newspaper, and pet–store bedding. They seemed not to care, as long as the material was soft and dry and covered them. Mice nest to hide and keep warm, and they will use any material that is soft, dry, and fluffy.

Tunnel or Hole?

Our mice liked to explore both tubes, but they seemed to really enjoy running through the open tunnel. In the wild, mice are always squeezing through cracks and holes.

Mice love to crawl through holes.

How Do Mice Prefer to Drink?

Our mice drank from all three sources. They seemed to prefer whatever source they were used to before the test. In the wild, mice get water wherever they find it—even rainwater or dew dripping from leaves. For pet mice, a water bottle is best, because they will often kick bedding into a dish or tip it over as they run around.

A wild mouse sips dew from a leaf. Its tail—dark above and light below—shows that it is a deer mouse.

Some Words About Mice

habitats Places where animals naturally live.

hibernate Spend the winter in a dormant, or resting, state.

home range The area an animal uses to meet its needs for food, water, and shelter.

mammals Animals that have fur, give birth to live young, and nurse their young with milk.

nocturnal Active during the night.

omnivorous Eating both animal and vegetable foods.

predators Animals that kill and eat other animals.

prey An animal that is caught and eaten by another animal.

rodents Animals with front teeth shaped like chisels, which they use for gnawing.

weaned No longer nursing.

A white–footed mouse raids a corn bin.

For More Information

Books

Richard Coniff, *Rats! The Good, the Bad, and the Ugly*. New York: Crown Books for Young Readers, 2002.

Sara Swan Miller, *Rodents: From Mice to Muskrats*. Danbury, CT: Franklin Watts, 1999.

Sally Morgan, *Rodents*. London: Chrysalis Education, 2004.

Stephen Savage, *Mouse*. London: Wayland, 2003.

Bradley Viner, *All About Your Mouse*. Hauppauge, NY: Barron's Educational Series, 1999.

Web Sites

A Kid's Guide to Basic Pet Rat & Mouse Care (www.afrma.org/kidsguide.htm). Tips from the American Fancy Rat & Mouse Association.

Rat and Mouse Club of America (www.rmca.org). Articles and other information, along with stories about a mouse that is a knight.

Index

aquarium, 25, 26

breeding, 16, 19
burrows, 21

cages, 27
cheek pouch, 21
climbing, 6, 13

deer mouse, 8–11, 16, 17
diseases, 20
drinking, 38–39, 44
droppings, 13

ears, 6, 8, 13, 14
eyes, 7, 8, 13, 14, 17

field mice, 14
food, 6, 8, 10–11, 13, 14,
    19, 20, 21, 22, 29
fur, 6, 8, 14, 17, 21

gnawing, 5, 20

grasshopper mice, 13

habitats, 4, 13
harvest mice, 14
hearing, 7
hibernation, 11
holes, 36–37, 43
home range, 10–11
house mouse, 11–13, 16,
    20, 25
houses, 26–27

jumping, 6, 13, 21

legs, 6, 21
litters, 16, 19, 25

mice
    body, 6–8
    care and handling,
        28–31
    color, 13, 14
    controlling, 20, 22

investigating, 32–44
life cycle, 16–19
and people, 20, 22–23
as pets, 24–31
size, 5, 13, 14, 17
types of, 8–14
mouse house, 26–27

nests, 7, 9–10, 14, 17, 21,
    33, 34–35, 41, 43
nocturnal creatures, 8, 9,
    24
nose, 6

offspring, 16–17
omnivores, 14

pests, 4, 23
pets, 23, 24–31
plant eaters, 8, 14
pocket mice, 21
predators, 7, 13, 19, 21
pups, 16–17, 25

rats, 5
rodents, 5

seedeaters, 14, 21
senses, 7
smell, 7

tail, 6, 8, 13, 14
teeth, 5, 13
tunnels, 36–37, 43

urine, 7

voles, 14

warm-blooded animals, 5
wastes, 17, 20
water, 21, 28, 38–39, 44
weaning, 17
whiskers, 7, 17
white-footed mouse, 8–11